CHAMPION SPORT

BIOGRAPHIES

CHAMPION SPORT

BIOGRAPHIES

MICHAEL BOUGHN

W

Warwick Publishing Inc.
Toronto   Los Angeles
www.warwickgp.com

We acknowledge the financial support of the Government of Canada through the Book Publishing Industry Development Program for our publishing activities.

ISBN: 1-894020-56-1

Published by Warwick Publishing Inc.
162 John Street, Suite 300, Toronto, Ontario, Canada M5V 2E5

Cover and layout design: Heidi Gemmill
Editorial Services: Joseph Romain

Printed and bound in Canada

Cover and interior photos courtesy AP/Wide World Photos

Table of Contents

Factsheet

Peter Sampras
Date of Birth: August 12, 1971
Place of Birth: Potomac, Maryland
Height: 6 feet 1 inch (185 centimetres)
Weight: 170 pounds (77 kilograms)
Plays: Right-handed

Career Highlights:
- Began playing tennis at age 7
- Changed from a two-handed to one-handed backhand in 1987
- Turned professional in 1988, ranked number 311 in the world
- Named ATP Player of the Year in 1993, '94, '95 and Jim Thorpe Tennis Player of the Year in 1993
- Won ESPY Award in 1994, 1995, and 1996
- Selected as one of "The 25 Fittest People in America" by *Fitness* magazine in 1994

Career Titles

1990	Philadelphia, Manchester, U.S. Open, Grand Slam Cup
1991	Los Angeles, Indianapolis, Lyon, ATP World Championships
1992	Philadelphia, Kutzbuhel, Cincinnati, Indianapolis, Lyon
1993	Sydney, Lipton, Tokyo, Hong Kong, Wimbledon, U.S. Open, Lyon, Antwerp
1994	Sydney, Australian Open, Indian Wells, Lipton, Osaka, Tokyo, Italian Open, Wimbledon, Antwerp, ATP World Championships
1995	Indian Wells, Queen's Club, Wimbledon, U.S. Open, Paris Indoor
1996	San Jose, Memphis, Hong Kong, Tokyo, Indianapolis, U.S. Open
1997	Philadelphia, San Jose Cincinatti, Grand Slam Cup, Paris, Australian Open, Wimbledon, ATP World Championship
1998	Advantas Championships, AT &T Challenge, Wimbledon, ATP World Championship, Paris

Introduction

The year 1990 didn't start out very well for Peter Sampras. Two years before, he'd dropped out of high school to go on the pro tennis circuit. Although his world ranking had risen to 81, his performance had been unsteady. He had placed second in the National Hard Court Championship in 1989, and had won the U.S. Pro Indoor in February of 1990. Then he hurt his hip and had to sit out of competition for two months.

More important, after two years as a pro, Sampras had yet to come close to winning his first Grand Slam event. Grand Slam events are the most important tournaments in the professional tennis circuit. Even though the other tournaments count towards a player's world ranking, they are considered to be warm-ups for the four Grand Slam competitions: the Australian Open, the French Open, Wimbledon, and the U.S. Open. After Sampras lost in the first round of Wimbledon play in June, 1990 looked like it wasn't shaping up to be much of a year.

Then came the U.S. Open. When Sampras went to Flushing Meadows, N.Y., to play the U.S. Open that summer, he was seeded 12th, which is to say he was ranked 12th best in the tournament. That doesn't sound bad, but it was well below the best players.

The previous year Sampras had lost in the second round of the U.S. Open, and even though he'd made it to the fourth round of the Australian Open in January, nobody, including Pete Sampras, expected him to do all that well. After all, he was only 19 years old.

Boy, were they in for a surprise.

One by one, his opponents fell to a spectacular serve and volley game that had finally come together for Sampras after years of work. A serve and volley game involves hitting lightning-fast serves and then rushing to the net to volley the ball if your opponent manages to return it.

And not many of Sampras's serves were getting returned. Since they were being clocked at around 125 miles per hour (200 km/h), that wasn't so surprising.

When Sampras beat Ivan Lendl in the quarterfinals, however, people really began to pay attention. It was the first time in nine consecutive years that Lendl hadn't made the U.S. Open finals. He'd won the Open three times and was one of the top-ranked players in the world.

Then Sampras went on to defeat former world champion John McEnroe in the semi-finals. That meant he would face Andre Agassi in the final match.

Agassi had defeated the defending U.S. Open champion Boris Becker in a four set match (to win a match, male players have to win the best of five sets). Sampras, playing the same serve and volley game that was to become his trademark, won three straight sets against a surprised Agassi, stunning the tennis world. Thirteen of his points were aces, serves that were so fast and well-placed that Agassi couldn't return them.

Pete Sampras was the youngest man ever to win the U.S. Open. Suddenly, his life changed forever. For one thing, he walked away from the U.S. Open with US$350,000 in his pocket. Not bad for a 19-year-old kid. From being ranked a lowly 81 in the world, he shot up to number 6. He was invited to play tennis with George Bush, then president of the United States. The media began to report on his life. Companies wanted him to represent their products.

But other less pleasant things happened, too. It was a bit like the old gunfighter scenario—Pete Sampras became the man to beat, and everybody was gunning for him.

Sampras found the combined pressure of his new fame and the ill feelings toward him difficult to bear. As he himself put it, "In 1990 I was immediately recognized all over the world. People were all over me and I don't like being the center of attention.

"It was from one extreme to the other, and for about six or eight months afterward I struggled with my life on and off the court. It was kind of a mess."

That's a lot of pressure on a 19-year-old kid who had come out of nowhere. People now expected him to keep winning. He wasn't prepared for that. And when he didn't win, people began to grumble that he didn't have what it takes to be number one, that he was a flash in the pan, that his U.S. Open win was just a stroke of luck.

Perhaps even harder for Sampras was the sudden exposure to all the gossip and backbiting that goes with fame. Sampras has always been a nice guy. His goal in tennis was to get past the childish and self-indulgent behavior that players like Jimmy Connors and John McEnroe had introduced into the game. Sampras wasn't interested in throwing temper tantrums—or tennis rackets. His hero was Australian Rod Laver, an old-time gentleman player.

You'd think people would find Sampras's attention to form admirable, but, on the contrary, Sampras now found himself criticized for being bland and boring. "Vanilla pudding," they called him.

The stress showed in his game. The victory in the U.S. Open was followed by a stunning series of defeats. Sampras won the Grand Slam Cup that December, but that wasn't considered an important tournament victory, even though he took home a two-million-dollar prize.

Sampras missed the next big Grand Slam tournament, the Australian Open, because of injuries. And then he only made it to the second round in both the French Open and Wimbledon. When he lost his U.S. Open title in the quarterfinals in 1992, people really began to talk.

Sampras didn't help matters. He was still basically a kid, and like most kids, he didn't always think before he talked. Before his U.S. Open defeat, he said in an interview that he felt like someone "carrying a backpack full of bricks around" after his upset victory.

Then when he lost the Open, he let it slip out that he felt "relieved." Many people could sympathize with that feeling, but others, including former champion Jimmy Connors, couldn't. Connors, who at 39 had just made it to the U.S. Open semi-finals, called it "the biggest crock I've ever heard, being 'relieved.'" Others said that if Sampras couldn't take the pressure, he should get out of the game.

It wasn't easy for a 20-year-old to hear that. Many other kids his age might have run away under those circumstances. Pete Sampras wasn't an ordinary kid, though. Summoning up the extraordinary resources that had led him to become the youngest U.S. Open champion in history, he doubled, then redoubled his effort.

Even so, it wasn't easy. Many losses, some of them heartbreaking, studded the years that followed. But Sampras never gave up, never slackened his effort.

In the long run it paid off. Sampras battled back to become one of the biggest winners in tennis. He has taken home tens of millions of dollars in prize money. He not only won the U.S. Open again, he won it another three times.

He also went on to win the Australian Open. He has won Wimbledon a spectacular six times. Only the French Open has eluded him, and with it his dream of winning all four titles in one year as his hero Rod Laver did. Still, no one doubts now that he has become one of tennis's all-time great players.

And if the past is any measure, no one can predict what Pete Sampras is yet capable of.

Chapter One

Beginnings

One day, when Peter Sampras was about six years old, he wandered into the basement of his family's house in Washington, D.C., looking for something to play with. Nobody could have predicted what eventually would come from that little adventure. What young Pete found was a long-abandoned tennis racket.

Pete picked the racket up and began to hit a ball with it. Soon he was spending hours hitting a ball against the basement wall. The thumping sound became a constant background noise in the Sampras house.

Pete Sampras was born on August 12, 1971. His father, Soterios "Sam" Sampras, was a second-generation American, the son of Greek immigrants. Sam was an engineer working for the Department of Defense. He also owned and ran a small restaurant. Pete's mother, Georgia, was born in Sparta in Greece, and had emigrated to the U.S.

Sam and Georgia met and got married in Potomac, Maryland, which is where Pete was born. Neither was very interested in playing tennis, so it was surprising when both Pete and his older sister, Stella, began to hit a tennis ball around. They quickly graduated from the basement to the courts at the local high school. But their interest didn't really take off until the family moved to California in 1978 when Pete was seven years old.

Tennis is a very popular sport in California, mostly because the weather there allows you to play outside year round. Moving from the east coast to the west coast would become an important event in Pete's development as a tennis player.

The Samprases moved to Palos Verdes, a small town not far from Los Angeles in sunny Southern California. Once there, both Pete and Stella began to play tennis more and more. Their father Sam decided to join a local tennis club—the Peninsula Racquet Club—and the kids quickly began playing tennis there as often as they possibly could.

Even at seven years of age Pete already showed a remarkable ability to hit a tennis ball. Sometimes when the Sampras kids went to the park to play, crowds would gather and discuss their abilities. One day while Sam was watching Pete and Stella, two strangers began talking to him about what an extraordinary player Pete was. They suggested that Sam find a tennis teacher to help Pete develop his game in a more serious and systematic way. Sam took their suggestion, and soon Pete was working with his first coach, Robert Lansdorf.

It wasn't long, though, before Sam decided that if Pete was to be a serious player, he would need more serious coaching. Pete was about nine years old at the time. It so happened that one of their acquaintances at the tennis club was a pediatrician—a child doctor—who taught tennis part time. Sam talked it over with Dr. Peter Fischer, and Fischer decided that he would coach the young tennis prodigy for free.

Dr. Fischer was Pete's first serious teacher. In many ways he can be credited with shaping the game that Pete has continued to play all his life.

For one thing, Fischer was a big fan of what is called the "serve-and-volley" game. This style of playing tennis involves serving the ball with a great deal of force and then rushing to the net. If your opponent manages to return the serve, the idea is to hit the ball back strongly before it touches your side of the court ("volley"). This kind of play tends to keep your opponent off balance and to allow you to score quick points. When it works, it's less tiring than long exchanges of groundstrokes from the backcourt, but it requires a very strong and reliable serve.

It also happened to be the favored game of Australian player Rod Laver. Laver, a champion during the 1960s, won the Grand Slam twice. Laver also represented tennis the way it was traditionally played. He was quiet and gentlemanly, unlike Americans Jimmy Connors and John McEnroe, who introduced a whole new rowdiness to the game in the 1970s and '80s. For the young Pete Sampras, Rod Laver was the ideal tennis player, and all his life Sampras has tried to be like his idol.

Pete and Paul Fischer worked together for ten years, starting when Pete was nine years old. By the time Pete was twelve years old, he says, he "was determined to be a tennis pro."

During those formative years, Pete played in the U.S. Tennis Association junior tournaments, where he usually ranked among the top 25 boy players. Among other people, he already was playing against Michael Chang, who would grow up to be both a friend and a competitor when they turned pro.

Sampras might have won more competitions, but Fischer had other concerns besides winning. His goal was to make Pete Sampras a champion by building strong fundamental skills. One of the ways he worked to achieve that was by matching Pete up with older, stronger players. That way the young player was never allowed to get too satisfied with himself. He always had to push a little further, a little harder, just to keep up with his opponents.

In 1985, Fischer made a crucial change in Pete's

game. Up until that time, he had used a two-handed backhand. That was the same backhand made popular by Chris Evert and Jimmy Connors a generation before. In fact, it was Pete's strongest stroke, and it was hard for him to give it up. Fischer insisted, however, because he thought Pete would have a longer reach and be able to get to more shots if he switched to one hand.

It was frustrating for Sampras, who was only 13 at the time. His ranking dropped from 25 to 56 after he started using the one-handed backhand. He lost games to players he knew he could have beaten if he had been playing his old game.

But with Fischer's encouragement, Pete stuck with it. After hundreds of hours of practice, the new stroke started to come together for him.

Fischer also had Pete spend countless hours working on his serve. Obviously, to develop a strong serve-and-volley game, the serve is crucial. He worked on three things: power, placement, and disguise. As Pete continued to grow, reaching six feet (183 cm) by the age of 15, his serve became more and more powerful.

It also became more controlled. He concentrated on being able to place the serve anywhere on the court. At the same time, he wanted to hide the ball's direction from his opponent, so Fischer had him work on using the same motion for all serves. Pete would throw the ball up and before he could hit it, Fischer would call out the kind of serve he wanted. Even Sampras didn't know what the serve would be until the last moment.

As his game came together under Fischer's direction, Sampras began to stand out among players his own age. He made the Boys' Junior Davis Cup team in 1987. He continued to play against his friend Michael Chang who was now the 18-and-under champion.

Sampras beat Chang in the U.S. Open Junior Boys' Championships, and then went on to place second in the National Hard Court Championships. He also won the 18-and-under International Grass Court doubles championship with partner Matt Lucena.

As Pete began to compete more and more successfully under the watchful eyes of his parents and his coach, they continued to guide him through the pitfalls of the game. Once, a few years earlier, Sampras had received what he thought was a bad call. In response he had thrown his racket at the fence. Jimmy Connors and John McEnroe had introduced this kind of brattish behavior to the game. Many young people, following the tennis stars' lead, began to throw their rackets and yell at officials, thinking that it was okay to act like that.

But both Sam Sampras and Peter Fischer agreed that such behavior was not acceptable. When the young Pete Sampras threw his racket, his father told him that if he ever did it again, he wouldn't be allowed to play. So Pete learned early how to behave properly on the court. The lesson has stuck with him to this day.

By the time he was 16 years old, Pete Sampras was beginning to attract the attention of many tennis watchers. Everyone agreed he had a remarkable natural ability. They also agreed that his skills and his attitude made him potentially one of the all-time top players in the game.

Playing tennis and going to school now began to conflict with each other in Pete's life. Having finished his junior year of high school, Pete and his coach began to talk about the possibility of his turning pro and going on the tennis circuit.

The professional tennis circuit is a yearly series of events anchored around the four Grand Slam Tournaments which occur in January (Australian Open), May (French Open), June-July (Wimbledon), and September (U.S. Open). Both Pete and his coach felt he was ready to turn pro, though dropping out of high school was not a choice Pete's parents favored. Still, in the end, Pete decided he was ready. Tennis meant everything to him. There was no point in delaying the inevitable.

In 1988, Pete Sampras took the plunge. He was 17 years old. His world ranking was 311.

Chapter Two

Taking the Plunge

If Pete Sampras thought he was going to jump into the pro circuit and make a big splash, he was in for a surprise. Even his detractors, if he had any at that point, probably wouldn't have predicted how ordinary his first year would be.

He didn't enter any of the major tournaments in 1988. He did reach the semi-finals in a match in Schenectady, New York, but generally his performance in the lesser events he did enter showed no signs of the greatness that was around the corner.

Late in 1988 he spent some time with champion Ivan Lendl at Lendl's home in Greenwich, Connecticut. Lendl, Sampras says, "had me biking twenty miles a day, talking to me about discipline and working hard and practicing until I couldn't walk home."

Lendl, who believed in a strict program of exercise and healthy food, impressed on Pete the importance of taking care of his body if he wanted to be a champion.

The advice seemed to work. Sampras's ranking slowly started to climb. By the end of 1988 he had reached 99, and early in 1989 he made it to 97. All through this period Sampras continued to work on honing his skills and increasing his concentration on the court. Concentration was a big issue for him, and he worked hard on it.

Meanwhile, the first big crisis in Pete's career was approaching. The relationship with his coach Dr. Peter Fischer was beginning to show signs of strain. There were disagreements over their financial arrangement. Fischer was also dissatisfied with Pete's effort. He felt Pete wasn't giving enough and wanted him to push himself harder in training.

Sampras in turn was dissatisfied with Fischer's inability to travel on the circuit because of his medical obligations. He felt that Fischer wasn't with him when he most needed him.

The disagreements between player and coach came to a head late in 1989 and the two men parted company, each blaming the other for the break up.

Sampras pushed ahead. He moved to Florida and hired a new coach, Joe Brandi, and a new trainer, Pat Etcheberry. Under the direction of Brandi and Etcheberry, Pete began to work out intensively, often in a hot garage. He wanted to build up a tolerance for extreme exertion in hot temperatures.

The results of his workouts began to show. At the

beginning of 1990 he was ranked 81. In January he made it to the semi-finals of the Australian Open. In February, he was back in the States in Philadelphia where he beat Andres Gomez in the finals at the U.S. Pro Indoor. It was his first professional title, and the first firm indication that all his hard training was beginning to pay off.

But then he hurt his hip and had to skip the French Open. After a couple of months recovering from the hip injury, Sampras went to Manchester, England, to play on grass courts in preparation for Wimbledon.

Tennis is played around the world on different surfaces. Most of Sampras's experience was on hard courts, which are widespread in California. In addition to hard courts, there are also clay courts, carpet-covered courts (which are a kind of hard court), and grass courts. Clay courts are prevalent in Europe, and grass courts in England. The French Open is played on clay and Wimbledon, England's most famous tournament, is played on grass. Balls play differently on each of the surfaces, so players who are serious about winning Grand Slam events have to develop different games for the different surfaces.

Things looked good for Sampras in England. He won his second professional title on the grass courts of Manchester. Given that victory, he hoped to do well on the grass courts at Wimbledon. Reeking with tradition, Wimbledon is probably the most well-known tennis tournament in the world. As Pete said later, "You can't do anything more in tennis than win Wimbledon, so I've always put a lot of emphasis on it. It's the biggest event on the tour."

His expectations, however, were short-lived in 1990. He lost in his first round at Wimbledon in straight sets to Christo Van Rensburg. It was a huge disappointment. Pete had not expected to win, but he hadn't counted on being defeated so thoroughly so quickly either.

It was a dejected Pete Sampras who returned to the U.S. that spring. He'd been on the pro circuit for almost two years and what did he have to show for it? There were a couple of minor titles. There were a few good matches. But what counted most to Pete Sampras were Grand Slam wins, and after two years, he still hadn't even come close to one of those. It was frustrating for the young athlete.

The next major tournament was the U.S. Open, which is played in Flushing Meadows, New York. Sampras began to prepare for it, doing intense daily training. By the time September rolled around, he felt he was ready. His serve was strong and as blisteringly fast as it had ever been. His groundstroke had come along. And he had mastered the running forehand shot that would become one of his trademarks, turning near disasters into triumphs.

Sampras went into the U.S. Open seeded 12th—

not bad, but certainly not among the top contenders. People began to realize something special was happening when, one by one, Pete's opponents fell before his powerful serve-and-volley game. By the time he got to the quarterfinals, the tournament was buzzing about the young man with the bushy eyebrows.

In the quarterfinals, Sampras went up against his friend Ivan Lendl. Lendl had made the finals of the U.S. Open for the last nine consecutive years. But he went down in the face of Sampras's sizzling serves, some of which were clocked at 125 mph (200 km/h). Next it was John McEnroe. McEnroe had won the Open four times, but Sampras took him out in four sets.

For the first time, Pete Sampras had made it to the finals of a Grand Slam tournament. Now he found himself going up against Andre Agassi. Agassi was 20 years old and ranked No. 4 in the world at the time. It was one of the first meetings between these two athletes whose competition in later years would become a media sensation.

In 1990, though, Agassi never stood a chance. Sampras had watched Agassi defeat defending champion Boris Becker earlier in the tournament. In that four set match, Agassi and Becker had spent most of their time in their backcourts trading long groundstrokes.

Watching them slug it out with each other, Sampras realized he had to avoid that kind of exhausting exchange. He knew that if he wanted to beat Agassi he had to serve hard and come to the net at every opportunity.

His strategy worked. Sampras came on strong, overwhelming Agassi with the unstoppable serve that was featured in headlines. He hit Agassi with 13 aces. The match was over in less than two hours as Agassi went down in three straight sets, 6-4, 6-3, 6-2.

"It was the best I could possibly play," Sampras said after the match, "and it couldn't have been at a better time. I controlled the match and dictated play. I don't know if anybody could have beaten me."

Even Agassi was impressed. "When you can hit a serve 120 mph on the line, there's not a lot you can do. This was just an old-fashioned street mugging," he joked.

Suddenly, Peter Sampras was a celebrity. He was the youngest man ever to win a U.S. Open title, and the lowest seed to win since unseeded Fred Stolle won in 1966. He was nicknamed "Pistol Pete" by the press for his powerful serve. He was in demand for interviews and T.V. appearances. He was even invited by then President George Bush to play doubles at the White House.

"I couldn't believe it," Sampras, said. "I was now part of an elite group. My name was going to be on that trophy with guys like Lendl and Becker and McEnroe and Connors and Laver. I couldn't believe that Pete

Sampras, a nineteen-year-old kid from California, was going to be on that trophy. Forever."

Things would never be the same again for Pete Sampras. Overnight his world ranking shot up from No. 81 to No. 6. Even more significant for the 19-year-old was the $350,000 in prize money he received.

One of the first things Sampras did after his victory was to call up his old coach, Dr. Peter Fischer. They had never made up after their parting of the ways. Pete knew that whatever their differences, he never could have gotten as far as he had without Fischer. He said so in an interview, pointing out how much he owed Fischer for his early guidance. The phone conversation was the opening that allowed them to begin patching up their relationship.

Sampras picked up another nickname in those first days of fame: "Sweet Pete." Many people found his pleasant and unassuming attitude refreshing after a decade of racket throwing and arguing by prominent American players. Sampras said his own goal was to present "a nice, clean-cut American image." Eventually, he would find that, once famous, even such a positive goal can become the basis for attacks by reporters hungry for sensation. But at the time, he was lavished with praise.

It was shortly after Pete's triumph at the U.S. Open that he began to discover some of the more negative aspects of being famous. About that time he began dating Delaina Mulcahy. Mulcahy was the ex-girl-friend of Sampras's former agent, Gavin Forbes. Their first date was a week-long vacation in Myrtle Beach, South Carolina.

Because Mulcahy was six years older than Sampras, and because they started seeing each other after his first big victory, they had to put up with gossip about how she was a cradle-robber or a gold-digger or both. It was as if having a real, loving relationship didn't make good headlines or sell advertising, so reporters had to start inventing scandals.

Sampras was a little surprised. "Your private life isn't private any more," he said in an interview with the *Washington Post*.

It's a bit curious that he didn't realize this kind of thing would happen when he got famous, but then, Pete Sampras was only 19 when he began to become well known.

Having won his first big title, Sampras was anxious to get out on the circuit and do it again. That December he played in the Grand Slam Cup. The Grand Slam Cup was a relatively new event. It was open only to the 16 players with the best records in the previous year's Grand Slam events.

While some people say it's really only a minor event in the world of tennis, its prize certainly isn't. When Sampras beat Brad Gilbert in the final, he walked away with a cool $2 million, $250,000 of which he donated to the cerebral palsy research foundation.

It seemed like the world belonged to Pete Sampras at the start of 1991. He was wealthy beyond his wildest dreams. He had an attractive girlfriend. He was the toast of the tennis world and a major American celebrity. Little did he know what the next few years held in store for him.

Pete Sampras was now the man to beat in the tennis world. Suddenly every player had to defeat Pete in order to prove himself. On top of that was the tremendous expectation of fans and the media that he would keep winning and winning and winning. When he didn't, it was like the roof fell in.

The next Grand Slam event after the U.S. Open was the Australian Open late in January. All eyes were on Sampras as the tournament approached. But Pete had to back out of the event. In December and January, he'd suffered numerous injuries—many more than usual—and so he was unable to play.

Then came the French Open, which is played on clay courts. For one thing, Sampras has never played very well on clay. But for another, the pressure seemed to show as well. Sampras went down in the second round in three straight sets to Thierry Champion.

As if that wasn't bad enough, the same thing happened at Wimbledon, though at least there Sampras won one set, losing to Derrick Rostagno in four.

Borrowing a phrase from his friend Michael Chang, Sampras described himself as "carrying a backpack full of bricks around" in the year since his upset victory at the U.S. Open. It was a tough haul for a kid not used to life in the limelight. Suddenly the same reporters who had been singing his praises a few months before began to suggest that Pete Sampras's U.S. Open victory in 1990 had been a fluke. He's a flash in the pan, they said, a one-shot-Johnny.

It only got more and more intense as the time for the 1991 U.S. Open drew near. Everyone waited to see if Sampras could duplicate his victory and defend his title.

The competition at the U.S. Open was fierce, but Sampras started out well. He took the first two rounds in straight sets, and easily defeated his relatively unknown opponents in rounds three and four in four sets.

When he reached the quarterfinals against Jim Courier, however, things collapsed. Sampras fought hard, but he seemed to lack motivation and his game never really came together. Courier just plain outplayed him. He even out-aced him, as Sampras went down 6-2, 7-6, 7-6.

It was bad enough that Pete lost his title. Then he had to go and open his mouth to the press about how he felt about losing.

"I'm kind of relieved," Sampras said honestly, not realizing how wimpy that would sound.

The uproar in response to this remark was furious, led by former champion Jimmy Connors. Connors, never known for his grace, lashed into Sampras.

"That's the biggest crock I've ever heard," Connors spat.

Even Pete's friend, Jim Courier, was taken aback by Sampras's statement. "Really," he said, "how much pressure does Pete have? He'll never have to work another day in his life. He's got millions in the bank and he's 20 years old."

Sampras ducked and ran for cover. He was completely inexperienced with the consequences of fame. He was used to being able to speak his mind. Suddenly nobody was giving him a chance to explain himself.

But such is the high-pressure life of professional sports, where the rewards are immense, but so are the demands. Pete learned his lesson. He hid out for a few weeks. Then in November, he was back.

Chapter Three

Fighting Back

If 1991 was a disaster of a year in terms of Grand Slam wins for Pete Sampras, 1992 wasn't a whole lot better.

He had finished up the 1991 circuit on a bright note. After his loss to Jim Courier in the U.S. Open, he looked forward to meeting him again in November at the Association of Tennis Professionals (ATP) World Championship in Frankfurt, Germany. This time he beat Courier in four hard-fought sets.

That pushed Pete's win-loss record for 1991 up to 36-6 since August. Not bad, all things considered. Sampras was playing well, but, unfortunately, not in the events that counted most.

Whatever consolation Sampras got from the victory over Courier was quickly lost when he joined the U.S. Davis Cup team for the final in France later that month. It was Sampras's first time in the Davis Cup competition. Still ranked No. 6 in the world, he was chosen by the U.S. team captain, Tom Gorman, along with Andre Agassi to represent the U.S. in singles competitions.

After Agassi won his opening match against French player Guy Forget, Sampras went up against Henri Leconte. Leconte wiped him out in straight sets in two hours and twenty-four minutes. Sampras looked every bit the 20-year-old kid away from home and not very sure of himself.

Things only got worse after that. Next Pete went up against Guy Forget. Admittedly it was hard for Sampras, having to play on an indoor court in front of 8,000 exuberant French fans who were not shy about letting Sampras know whose side they were on. It was a new experience for the 20-year-old kid from California, and not one he enjoyed.

To make matters worse, Forget was at the top of his game, cheered by the same crowd that jeered Sampras. He overwhelmed the young American, serving 17 aces and beating him in four sets.

With that loss, France won the Cup. And Sampras had to bear the responsibility for the U.S.'s loss. "I just wasn't ready," he said later.

Sampras decided not to play in the Australian Open in January 1992. Instead, he made an important change to his training team, hiring Tim Gullikson to be his coach. Gullikson and his twin brother Tom had played the pro circuit for years in the 1970s and knew the game of tennis inside out.

The first thing Gullikson did was get Sampras working on his groundstroke. Sampras's serve was still one of the fastest in the game, but he had never put the same kind of effort into perfecting his ground-strokes. If he didn't win off the serve, he sometimes found himself at a disadvantage playing in the back-court.

Sampras threw himself whole-heartedly into learning the new techniques, and soon the work paid off. Sampras's backcourt game started to improve noticeably. One of the first places it showed up was when he went back into Davis Cup play. Immediately he led the U.S. team first-round wins over two Argentineans. It was a sweet victory for Sampras after the embarrassment of the previous fall.

Next came the French Open and the clay courts that had plagued Sampras during his career. Tim Gullikson hoped that if Sampras could significantly improve his groundstrokes it would help his clay court game. Clay courts were bad news for Sampras because the ball plays much slower on clay than on the hard court surfaces Sampras grew up with. That means that players had more time to get in position to return his serve and he found himself playing in the backcourt more often. A stronger groundstroke meant a stronger clay court game.

"I understand that it takes 20 to 30 balls on clay to win a point," Sampras said, "and I don't mind staying back and trading groundies. Playing on clay takes a much more intense mentality, and you have to be more willing to grind it out."

It seemed that all the hard work was paying off. When Sampras came to France in the spring of 1992, he was much heartened to sweep through the first four rounds, losing only one set in the first round match to Marc Rosset. For the first time he was a contender. He looked strong going into the quarterfinals. But not strong enough to overcome Andre Agassi, who beat him in three straight sets, 7-6, 6-2, and 6-1.

In June it was off to Wimbledon, and a whole different surface: grass. So far Pete had had only one victory on the grass at Wimbledon. That had been the year before when he'd beaten Danilo Marcelino in the first round.

But Sampras had high hopes in 1992, mostly because of Gullikson, his coach. As players, Gullikson and his brother had reached the Wimbledon doubles finals one year, and another year Tim had scored an upset victory over John McEnroe.

Gullikson knew that Sampras had it in him to win the English tournament, but before he could get there, he'd have to work on his return. Everyone agreed that the return was the crucial stroke on Wimbledon's grass, and that Sampras's just wasn't good enough.

Gullikson had a number of ideas about how Pete could make his return stronger. He had him shorten his stroke slightly and play the ball rather than waiting for it to play him.

One of the most important problems Gullikson identified was attitude. Because the grass amplified the power of serves, aces were a fact of life for everyone. While Pete had no problem dishing out aces, he tended to get a bit depressed when he was on the receiving end of them. The more Sampras learned to just accept the aces scored on him, the stronger his game got.

And in 1992, it showed. In the three previous years he had played Wimbledon, Sampras had never gotten past the second round. But in 1992, he blew through the first four rounds. Only the second round match against Todd Woodridge went to more than three sets, and that took only four.

In the quarterfinals Pete had his toughest opponent yet. Michael Stitch had won the tournament the previous year. But in 1992 he was completely outclassed by Sampras. Pete beat him in three straight sets, losing only nine games.

That put him into the semi-finals against Croatian Goran Ivanisevic. Ivanisevic was hot. He was burning aces like they were going out of style. Though Pete had been working on his attitude towards returning serves, it suddenly all seemed to come apart when he was faced with Ivanisevic's power.

"I had so little chance to return serves," Pete said

later, "that I got really down on myself." As he admitted after the match, "I just bailed out."

Losing in four sets was a tremendous disappointment to Sampras. And not just because he had lost Wimbledon again after such a strong start. This was the sixth Grand Slam event since his surprise victory at the U.S. Open, and he had failed to win a single one of them. Even Sampras must have had moments when he wondered whether or not his one Grand Slam win was a fluke.

Still, there were other victories, even if they weren't necessarily the victories he was most hungry for. From Wimbledon he went to Austria where he won his first Austrian clay court match. The fact that it was a clay court made the win all the sweeter. From there it was back to the States and a couple of hard court victories, in Cincinnati against Ivan Lendl and in Indianapolis against Jim Courier.

In the summer of 1992, the Olympic Games were to be played in Barcelona, Spain. Sampras had been selected for the U.S. team. Once again he'd be playing on clay, a prospect he looked forward to with mixed emotions. Even though he'd won in Austria, clay continued to be a problem for him. As it turned out, the Olympics were no exception. He went down in the third round of singles competition. And when he and Jim Courier played doubles against the Spanish, they lost, even though they had been up 2-0.

Then suddenly it was September and time for the U.S. Open again. It had been two years since "Sweet Pete" had pulled off his surprise upset—in some ways, two very tough years. He had yet to win another Grand Slam title, and as a result he still had to put up with the doubters and the gossips whispering how he wasn't really a champion.

But it wasn't as if he wasn't winning. By the end of 1992, he would have a 70-18 record for the year, and he would earn over a million dollars in prize money. Not bad for somebody who was supposedly out of his league.

Still, Sampras knew that in the long run, it was only the Grand Slam events that counted. He could win all the minor tournaments in the world, but when the records were all tallied up, only the four big ones really meant anything. No matter how you looked at it, being back in Flushing Meadows, N.Y., was a big deal.

Sampras came on strong at the U.S. Open. He breezed through the first two rounds. Then, in the third round, against Todd Martin, down two sets to one, he fought back, winning the last two and taking the match. The previous year, he told the press after the match, he probably wouldn't have been able to do that.

After Martin came Pete's French Davis Cup nemesis, Guy Forget. But this time they were playing on Sampras's home turf. Forget fought hard and had

Sampras down 2-1 after three sets, but again Pete fought back to take the match in 5. It was an important match because, as Sampras pointed out afterward, he hadn't been playing his best, but he still pulled through. This was a new Sampras.

"I'm not sure I'm going to win the tournament," he said. "I'm not playing that great right now, but I'm fighting and winning. That's important to me."

Excitement really began to build when he wiped out Alexander Volkov, 6-4, 6-1, 6-0, in the quarterfinals, and advanced to the semi-finals against Jim Courier.

Courier, though, was no pushover like Volkov had been. He fought hard.He couldn't stop Sampras, however, who took the match in four sets. It was an important victory for Sampras, one that he paid a physical price for, coming out of it suffering from dehydration and cramps. That victory set him up for the final against Stephan Edberg.

Finally Sampras was back in the finals of the U.S. Open, the site of his great upset two years before. Everyone wondered whether he could do it again. Edberg was no pushover, either, even though he'd just gone through an exhausting three consecutive five-set matches.

But the match against Courier had taken it out of Sampras, too. Even worse, he came down with the flu that weekend and had to receive medical treatment. Pete might have backed out of the match, but he didn't.

It was a moment where what counted was sheer strength of both body and character. Sampras had a lot to prove after his ill-considered remarks of the previous year. At that time he had seemed happy to give up his crown. Now he wanted nothing more than to win it back and prove that he was worthy. And neither physical exhaustion nor severe illness were going to hold him back.

But it wasn't to be, not this year, anyway. After splitting the first two sets, Stephan Edberg took the third in a tough tiebreaker that seemed to suck the juice right out of Sampras. After that, his serve fell apart, and Edberg easily took the last set 6-2.

It was a tough loss for Pete, especially after having fought so hard to get to the finals again. With the defeat, Edberg moved to No. 1 in world rankings, and Sampras fell to No. 3.

The two men met again in December in Davis Cup doubles competition. Paired with John McEnroe, Sampras took on the team of Edberg and Anders Jaryd, defeating them in a hard-fought, five-set match, after being down two sets to nothing. After Sampras's disappointing Davis Cup play in 1991, the victory encouraged him. The fact that it was against Edberg probably counted for something, too.

As the 1992 season came to a close, things didn't look too bad for Pete Sampras. He had won five titles and seventy matches worth $1.5 million. That was more than any other professional male player. And not bad take-home pay for a 21-year-old, either. Even Sampras's clay record was showing definite signs of improvement. Out of thirty sets in 1992, he had won twenty-seven in eight tournaments.

Other important things were going on in Pete's life, too. His girlfriend Delaina Mulcahy had enrolled in law school at Stetson University in St. Petersburg, Florida. It was a move that Sampras supported.

"I don't feel any sort of guilt because she's in law school," he said. "I've always told her she's got to do what she wants to do and not be dependent on me. . . . I think it's really great for our relationship that she has her own agenda. That's really important."

In December of 1992 Sampras bought a house for Delaina and himself with his earnings. The house was a 7,862-square foot (731 m²) monster in an exclusive Tampa neighborhood called Tampa Palms. The house cost Sampras $700,000. The pool and patio alone covered 2,000 square feet (186 m²)—plenty of room for Pete and Delaina and their two dogs.

But Sampras was still haunted by one overriding fact: He hadn't picked up a single Grand Slam title all year. In fact, he hadn't won one since his U.S. Open victory in September 1990. That was beginning to seem like a long time ago.

Chapter Four

Wimbledon Wonder

It was pretty obvious early in 1993 that Pete Sampras's game was turning around—finally. He was spending a lot of time with Tim Gullikson and his trainer, Pat Etcheberry, working on improving his conditioning. He'd been plagued by injuries in 1992, especially shin splints and shoulder problems, and wanted to avoid those problems in the future. Gullikson was also pushing Sampras to continue working on his ground-stroke and his service return. Gullikson considered them to be the two weak points in Sampras's game.

Pete had missed the Australian Open because of injuries in 1991. He'd missed it for the same reason in 1992. When it rolled around again in 1993, he went there with one goal in mind: to win the tournament and take the No. 1 world ranking away from Jim Courier.

He made a good beginning, rising quickly to the semi-finals. Of the five matches he played to get there, only one went to four sets. The rest he won easily in three straight sets. In the semi-finals, though, he ran smack up against Stephan Edberg, who turned the tables on him, beating him in three. It was a tremendous disappointment for Sampras.

From there it was off to Japan, where Pete finally won the title by beating Brad Gilbert in the final. That victory pushed his overall record up enough to nudge him past Jim Courier and into first place in world ranking.

His hold was not firm, however, and tennis circles were abuzz with arguments about whether Sampras deserved the promotion. Many people felt that since he hadn't won a major tournament since 1991, he didn't belong in the No. 1 position.

The debate only got more intense when Sampras lost to Andre Agassi in the quarterfinals of the French Open a few months later. Once again he was the victim of clay. He just couldn't seem to win on clay courts, no matter how much he worked on his game. The skeptics argued that he was just too limited a player to deserve No. 1 ranking.

That certainly increased the pressure on Pete as Wimbledon approached. Of all the Grand Slam tournaments, Wimbledon meant the most to Sampras. It might have had something to do with his first coach. Pete Fischer had always stressed Wimbledon as Sampras's utmost goal.

In fact, Fischer later admitted that was why he had convinced Sampras to give up his two-handed back-stroke all those years ago. Fischer had already been thinking about Wimbledon, and the two-handed backhand was interfering with the development of the serve and volley game necessary to win the English title.

Wimbledon has always been deeply involved in the tradition of the game of tennis, and that appealed to Pete as well. He had always seen himself as a traditional player, as someone defending and renewing the traditions of the game.

"It starts when you walk through the gate," Sampras said. "You really feel the character of Centre Court and the character of the grounds. It's just different from any other Grand Slam tournament we play."

It didn't start off well for Sampras. He flew to England a week early to spend some time playing tennis with Elton John at John's estate in Windsor. Tendinitis flared up in his right shoulder only a few days before the tournament was to begin. Sampras's trainer, Pat Etcheberry, worked hard to get the shoulder in shape so he could play.

The year 1993 was an important one in the history of Wimbledon. It was the 100th anniversary of the tournament. Many people turned out to celebrate the centenary of the venerable competition. The crowds were excited, the Centre Court stands full of celebrities. Princess Diana was there, and the American singer and actor Barbara Streisand, who had just started a relationship with Andre Agassi. More important for Pete, Delaina Mulcahy was there, too, having flown over from the U.S. to cheer her boyfriend on.

Sampras won the first four sets easily in spite of his shoulder. Playing against England's Andrew Foster in the fourth round, Pete got a taste of the crowd's—and the media's—hostility towards him. The audience openly cheered for Foster and expressed displeasure when Sampras scored points. If he thought it was bad then, he had no idea what was in store for him.

In the next round—the quarterfinals—Pete found himself going up against another American, Andre Agassi. Agassi had developed a flamboyant style that was extremely popular with the crowds. It was exactly the opposite of Pete's low-key style. Pete appealed to tradition. He wore white and pastels. Agassi wore bright colors and had long hair held back in a ponytail. Just before their match, a poll had named Agassi the most popular athlete in England.

The match was a tough one. Sampras's shoulder started acting up. Up two sets, Sampras then lost the next two. During the fifth set, he had to stop play briefly to get his shoulder massaged. He managed to hang in though, beating Agassi 6-4 to take the match.

After the match a British reporter told Pete he was now the most unpopular man in England. That was hardly the response Sampras had expected. But it did not slow him down. He went on to beat Boris Becker in the semi-final in straight sets, mainly because of his serve. This advanced him to the final where he would play Jim Courier in the first all American Wimbledon final since McEnroe and Connors played in 1984.

At the time, Sampras and Courier were ranked No. 2 and No. 1 in world, so it was truly to be a battle of champions. The first two sets established the tone. Seesawing back and forth, both sets went to tiebreakers. Pushing himself to the limit, Sampras managed to edge Courier out 7-6 in both. Then Sampras seemed to lose steam. Courier came on strong taking the third set, 6-3.

But Sampras found new reserves. Calling on everything Tim Gullikson had been teaching him, Sampras stayed back and exchanged long groundstrokes with Courier. He pulled ahead 4-2 in the fourth set, eventually winning it with his serve, 6-3.

Pete Sampras was now the Wimbledon champion. His dream had come true at last.

Even more important, he had finally won another Grand Slam event. If anyone still had doubts about who was No. 1 in the world, they had to keep their mouths shut now—at least about that. But another controversy immediately erupted in the British press after Pete's victory. The headline in the *Daily Mirror* read, "It's Pete Samprazzzz: Bored on the Fourth of

July." "Pete's A Bore," another paper announced. Still a third proclaimed, "Tennis is no longer sweet music. Power has corrupted its spirit," a comment on Sampras having served 22 aces in his match with Courier. Another called him a "gloomy robot."

It seems hard to believe that legitimate newspapers would raise a ruckus about a tennis player being too polite. But the British tabloids are not known for their restraint. And they achieved their goal, setting off a debate about Sampras's personality, and whether in fact personality has anything to do with athletics.

Though it must have been a bit strange for Pete, the bottom line was, he didn't care. He didn't have to. He had won Wimbledon. He had proven once and for all that his 1990 U.S. Open victory was no fluke. He was No. 1.

But not, unfortunately, for long. Exhausted after Wimbledon, Sampras went on to lose some lesser tournaments in early rounds. When he lost the U.S. Men's Hard Court title in Indianapolis that summer, he slipped back to No. 2 ranking, once again trailing Jim Courier. Recovering his No. 1 ranking became his most important goal, so when he was asked to be part of the U.S. Davis Cup team again, he declined. He needed to stay focussed on the task at hand.

He went into the U.S. Open that autumn with a lot at stake—his ranking, for one thing. But even beyond that was the question of whether, having won

Wimbledon, he could do it again. As his coach Tim Gullikson pointed out, "Pete has a real hunger to stay at the top."

To top it off, this was the tournament where it had all begun for him three years before. Even with the Wimbledon win, Pete was still smarting from the furore that had followed his ill-conceived comments following his loss of the U.S. Open title in 1991. If he had been relieved to give up his title then, he would be more than relieved to win it back now and prove that he had what it takes to be a champion.

Pete knew he was in good shape to win the title back. What he didn't know was that the toughest match of the game would be his quarterfinal bout against his old friend Michael Chang.

The two men had grown up playing tennis against each other. Their first match had been in a 10-and-under competition in San Diego in 1980, and over the years they'd gone head to head many times. As often as not, Chang was the winner. He had beaten Pete in several minor tournaments, as well as the 1989 French Open, which he took in straight sets. He had won six of their eight matches on the pro tour that year.

That Wednesday night in 1993, it was by no means certain who was going to win. The first two sets went to tiebreakers. Sampras took the first 6-7, but Chang fought back to take the second 7-6. Chang had Sampras running all over the court.

Inspired by his competition, Pete finally found his groove and started firing lightning-bolt shots that scored from wherever he hit them. Even though the last two sets look lop-sided—6-1, 6-1, for Sampras— they were extremely hard fought. Many of the spectators described it as the best tennis they had ever seen.

After the match a reporter asked Chang what he could have done to beat Sampras. "What could I do?" Chang replied. "I don't know. . . . maybe go over and snap his strings. There's really nothing you can do. When he's playing his best, he's practically unbeatable."

And there was no question Pete was playing his best. After the grueling match against Chang, things went a bit easier for Sampras. In fact, the rest of the tournament was a snap by comparison. In the semi-finals, Russian Alexander Volkov went down in straight sets with no fuss. Sampras then went up against Cedric Pioline.

Pioline was the first Frenchman in 61 years to make the U.S. Open finals. He had beaten Jim Courier and Wally Masur to get there. The press made a big deal about it. But when push came to shove, Michael Chang had called it. Pioline went down under Pete's blistering serve in three easy sets.

It was a sweet moment for Pete Sampras. In one stroke he regained his No. 1 world ranking and his U.S. Open title. He was no longer the kid he had been just two years before, uneasy under the burden of his sudden fame. Now he knew what he wanted—really knew—and he had gotten it.

He was also the first American in nine years to take both Wimbledon and the U.S. Open in succession. What's more, he was the first male player to serve more than 1,000 aces in a year. Sampras had served 1,011 to set a new world record.

It hadn't been a bad year financially either. The 1993 U.S. Open prize was $535,000. Added to the rest of his winnings for the year, it brought Pete's total prize money to more than $3.6 million. In addition, he brought home a total of eight titles.

After winning the Open, Sampras headed home to spend some time with Delaina, who was studying for her law degree. They were still living together in the Tampa house Sampras had bought the previous year.

In addition to tennis, Sampras's success meant he had other responsibilities as well. The more he won, the more product-endorsement offers he had. Apart from tennis equipment, he was asked to represent sunglasses, shoes, and clothing. His endorsement income was bringing him another $2 million a year on top of his prize money.

Still, as 1994 approached, Pete's mind was mostly on tennis, not money. Winning two successive Grand Slam tournaments had put him in a special position—halfway to the Grand Slam. There was still a long way to go—especially considering the road ran through the clay courts of the French Open—but there was no way to avoid thinking about it. For one thing, everyone was talking about it. For another, Pete's idol, Rod Laver, had done it not just once, but twice, and Pete always thought about that.

But it wouldn't be easy. Four tournaments in four climates on four different surfaces was a challenge only the greatest tennis players had succeeded at. Was Pete Sampras good enough to join their ranks?

No one could say for sure. But in 1994, he would have a shot at it.

Pete Sampras puts every-
thing into returning the ball
during a match at the US
Open in 1996.

Pete reaches for a shot during the men's singles semi-finals at Wimbledon in 1998.

Pete Sampras gets ready to make one of his killer serves during a match at the 1997 Australian Open.

Pete celebrates his victory over Goran Ivanisevic in the men's singles final at Wimbledon in 1998. It was the fifth time Sampras had won the famous tennis contest.

Chapter Five

Superstar on a Roll

Certainly one of the things Pete Sampras didn't think he'd have to worry about in 1994 was the accusation he was ruining tennis. But he did.

Just at a time when his reputation as a tennis player was taking off around the world, Pete had to admit that some people thought he was too good—too good a tennis player and too nice a guy. His serve was so strong that many tennis observers felt Sampras was taking the joy out of the game. He was accused of steamrolling his opponents.

At the same time, his supposed sweet temper and good nature were seen as too boring. It may seem strange now to look back at that moment and realize people were serious. But it was the age of Dennis Rodman, the flamboyant basketball player. Apparently some people felt tennis needed a similar figure to liven up the game.

Pete tried to put these criticisms behind him as he readied himself for the first Grand Slam event of 1994, the Australian Open. He came to Melbourne with a lot of hopes—and a lot of baggage. At 22, he was ranked No. 1 and held a huge lead in ATP Tour rankings. Having won the two previous Grand Slam events, comparisons between him and previous champions were being tossed around in the press. Whether he could live up to all the talk was another question.

He was seeded first at the tournament, but it wasn't an easy go for him. The second round match against Russian Yevgeny Kafelnikov was a tough one, and Pete almost lost it. Kafelnikov was hot. Frequently his ground shots zipped by Sampras, who stood at the net looking surprised. After taking the first set 6-3, Sampras lost the second 2-6. He then came back to win the third 6-3, only to collapse in the fourth, which Kafelnikov took 1-6. It all came down to the fifth set, which turned into a brutal tiebreaker. Sampras finally took it 9-7, winning the match.

After that it was much smoother sailing for Sampras. He beat Stephane Simian, Ivan Lendl, Magnus Gustafsson, and Jim Courier to advance to the finals against Todd Martin. He felt he was in good shape to take the Australian title for the first time.

Jim Courier agreed. When asked what strategy might work against Pete, Courier quipped, "Maybe break his leg on the changeover."

The night before their showdown, Martin and Sampras had dinner together. But the next day they were ready to battle. It was Sampras all the way as he rolled over Martin in three straight sets, taking the Australian Open title and his third straight Grand Slam event. It had been 30 years since another man had done that—Roy Emerson, who won three in row in 1964–65.

The buzz around Sampras became all the more intense as the French Open neared. Everyone wondered out loud whether Sampras could win it for the overall Grand Slam title. Various sportswriters compared him positively and negatively to the great champions of the past.

Even some of those champions joined in the chorus of voices. Rod Laver, Sampras's hero and a two-time Grand Slam winner, published an article in *Tennis* magazine called "How Sampras Can Win the French." He suggested that Pete back off a bit on his serve, go after returns a bit more, and get to the net even more than he already did. He also recommended that Pete avoid talking about the whole Grand Slam phenomenon in order to keep some of the pressure off.

In the midst of all the excitement, Pete tried to keep focussed on the task at hand. But there was intense pressure from the press to talk about the possibility of the big win. Sampras downplayed all the hype as best he could and just kept on playing tennis.

The months leading up to the French Open were rewarding ones. Sampras dominated the tour, winning 27 consecutive matches. He even won the Italian Open title for the first time, beating Boris Becker on clay. This was only his second clay court victory. Under other circumstances it wouldn't have been a big deal. But with everyone madly speculating on whether he could win in France given his weakness on clay courts, his Italian win further fueled the fires. Sampras was still cautious.

"I'm getting better," he said, "but it is definitely going to be a huge challenge for my game on that surface."

At the beginning of a tournament, players draw their opponents for the first rounds. Going into the French Open, Sampras was hoping for an easy draw, but he didn't get it. His first round opponent, Alberto Costa, was a 19-year-old Spaniard who had been named Newcomer of the Year in the 1994 ATP tour. Costa played good tennis, but Sampras won in straight sets.

That set him up to play an 18-year-old Chilean named Marcelos Rios. Rios, too, was an up-and-coming player. He'd been ranked No. 1 boy player in 1993. But he also went down in straight sets, although two went to tiebreakers.

Pete's third round opponent, Dutchman Paul Haarhuis, was a tough player with a reputation for beating champions. But by that time Sampras was coming on strong. The clay seemed to be no problem for him as he defeated Haarhuis in three sets, too.

But in the fourth round, Pete's game started to show some rough edges. Playing Mikael Tillstrom, Sampras took two sets, then started to lose it. He dropped the third set 6-1, and had to scramble in the fourth set to pull out the match. Still, even if it was rough, it was a win, and he advanced to the quarterfinals against his old opponent, Jim Courier.

Even though Sampras led Courier 10-2 in their overall record, they had never met each other on clay before. And whereas Pete had always struggled with clay, Courier was quite at home on it. The difference showed in the match, as Sampras's Grand Slam hopes went down in flames. Courier was all over him as the clay nullified Sampras's power. Relying on his strong groundstroke game, Courier took the match in four sets.

The loss was extremely disappointing for Pete. He was still ranked No. 1 in the world, but his run was over, along with his hopes for a Grand Slam. Now he'd have to start all over again.

And what better place to do it than Wimbledon, his favorite tournament. The year before, his Wimbledon win had broken his Grand Slam losing streak, and started him on his run for the Grand Slam. This year he was coming into the tournament as the defending champion with four Grand Slam titles to his name, and if the Brits still thought he was boring, well, that was their problem.

Pete wasn't about to alter his winning game to make the English press happy. In the first match with Jared Palmer, Sampras aced his opponent 25 times in three sets. It was Sampras at his most menacing. He kept it up, sweeping the next two matches in straight sets.

The press ignored him, however, preferring to print stories about American player Katrina Adams' colorful underwear.

Beating Michael Chang in the quarterfinals, Sampras advanced to the semis against Todd Martin. Martin had beaten Sampras a couple of weeks before in the Queen's Cup final. At Wimbledon, during their third set, Sampras stumbled while hitting a forehand shot and twisted his ankle. He walked it out, but lost the set—the first he'd lost in the tournament.

But Pete came back to take the match and advance to the finals against Goran Ivanisevic, who had replaced Jim Courier in the No. 2 spot in world rankings. The first two sets went to tiebreakers, but Sampras's strength led him to 7-6 victories. After that, Ivanisevic collapsed, and Sampras swept the third set 6-0 in 19 minutes.

Pete Sampras had successfully defended his Wimbledon title. The British press had better get used to him, he seemed to be saying.

"People can write what they want and when they want," he said, "but the fact is I've got two Wimbledons in a row and that's going to stay with me." He planned to be around for a while.

Even though he had lost the French Open, Pete Sampras was clearly still on roll. He was easily holding on to his No. 1 world ranking. In addition, *Tennis* magazine voted him Player of the Year and he received the Tennis Award from the Jim Thorpe Association.

However, the effort to win took a toll on him physically. When he left England after Wimbledon he headed to the Netherlands to play in the Davis Cup competition on hard courts. Pete's ankle, weakened when he twisted it in England, got worse with all the pounding in took on the hard courts. Tendinitis developed.

The injury was serious enough that Sampras was forced to withdraw from four consecutive tournaments between Wimbledon and the U.S. Open. Those included the hard court games in Cincinnati and Indianapolis that are part of the lead-up to the U.S. Open in September.

Pete stayed in Tampa with Delaina. He did what he could to keep up his overall condition without further straining his ankle. But his conditioning was deteriorating daily. Then, just when he thought the ankle was getting better, another pain developed in it.

Doctors found that a calcium deposit had formed. That was two days before the beginning of the U.S. Open. Even though he was working out with Stephan Edberg and Tim Gullikson, his ankle stiffened.

Sampras tried to play the injury down. "I think I'm more or less back on track," he said before the Open. But it was pretty clear that he wasn't in top form.

He went into the tournament as defending champion, and he looked it, too, in the beginning. He took the first two matches without many problems. But by the third set, his lack of conditioning began to show. Playing against Roger Smith, Sampras dropped the first set, but then came back to win the next three. That set him up for a fourth-round match against Jaime Yzaga, an unseeded player from Peru.

It's a match many see as one of Sampras's best, even though he lost. Yzaga took the first set, then Sampras came back. The third set went to Yzaga again, and the fourth to Sampras in a brutal tiebreaker, 7-6. By the fifth set, Sampras was beginning to show the strain. He increasingly had to struggle for wind between points.

By then the match had gone on for almost three hours. Sampras was clearly struggling. He had developed blisters. His weak ankle was sore. His back was cramping.

But he wouldn't give up. It was a Pete Sampras no one had seen before. He fought and fought. The match went to three and a half hours before Yzaga was finally able to finish Sampras off 7-5 in the last set.

After the match, Yzaga told the press, "He never gave up. I congratulate him. Obviously he wasn't feeling well, but that's what makes him a champion. He kept fighting until the end."

After being treated by doctors for dehydration, Sampras spoke to the press, too. "I figured that if he was going to beat me, I wanted him to go the distance," he said. "I wasn't going to retire and let him not earn it."

Sampras may have lost his title, but everyone agreed he was more of a champion than ever.

And he was still No. 1. Even with his U.S. Open loss, Pete still had a strong enough record to hold on to his world ranking. All in all, 1994 hadn't been a bad year. The disappointment of his losses in the French Open and the U.S. Open was certainly real. But he had defended two major titles and another four minor ones. In fact the only title from 1993 that he had lost was the U.S. Open. There was no question in anyone's mind that Sampras was still a winner.

Chapter Six

Struggling with Grief

The year 1995 did not start out well for Pete Sampras. Late the previous year, Delaina Mulcahy had been in a car wreck. Although her injuries weren't too serious, it shook Sampras up. Then, his friend and coach, Tim Gullikson, the man credited with helping him become a champion, had become ill. In October Gullikson had collapsed in a hotel room in Stockholm, falling onto a table and gashing open his nose.

After that, Gullikson went to a series of different doctors who gave him different explanations of what was wrong. Doctors in Illinois said it was a faulty heart valve. Doctors in Germany, where he had another attack several months later, said it was strokes. Everyone agreed that whatever it was, it was serious.

While Sampras had held on to his No. 1 ranking in 1994, he had ended the year on a down note. Not only had he lost the U.S. Open title, but after that he'd gone to Sweden to play in the Davis Cup and had hurt himself, pulling a hamstring. He'd had to drop out of the competition and watch as the Swedes beat the American team. To make matters worse, it was the first time that a title was lost because a player withdrew, and even though Sampras had had no choice, he had to live with that knowledge.

He started the new season with high hopes, his sights set on the Australian Open title that he had successfully held for two years in a row. He was doing well, too, having easily advanced to the third round, when disaster struck.

On January 20, after a workout with Pete, Tim Gullikson passed out again. He was rushed to hospital and examined by doctors who came up with another diagnosis: brain cancer. They gave him six months to live.

Before rushing to the hospital to be with his friend, Sampras won his third round match. But it wasn't an easy win. He lost the first two sets and had to struggle to regain his concentration, battling back to win the last three sets.

For the next several rounds of the tournament, Pete spent all the time he wasn't on the court at the hospital. Finally, Gullikson was flown back to the United States, leaving Sampras without a coach and in a distressed state of mind.

Pete found himself in the quarterfinals playing

against Jim Courier. Courier was on a hot streak that January. He took the first two sets from Sampras in tiebreakers. Sampras, visibly struggling, managed to win the next two. By that time, on top of everything else, he'd developed painful blisters on his feet. Going into the fifth set, a fan, hoping to encourage him, yelled out, "Do it for your coach!"

It was more than Sampras could take, and at the changeover, he burst into tears while the whole world watched on TV. Splashing cold water on his face, he struggled to go on. He broke into tears again and stood on the court sobbing.

Delaina Mulcahy quietly urged him from court-side to go on. Jim Courier offered to postpone the rest of the match till the next day. But Sampras elected to play on and, firing serves through his tears, aced out Courier, winning the fifth set and the match.

After a four-set semi-final victory over Michael Chang, Sampras told the press: "I think people under-stand that I'm normal, that I have feelings like every-one else, that I'm not a robot out there; that I play the way I play and the way I carry myself is just the way I am. I'm as normal as anyone else. This was a very tough thing to go through."

And it didn't get any less tough. Going into the final to defend his title, Sampras found himself play-ing against Andre Agassi, the man who had won the U.S. Open the previous fall. Agassi had just overhauled his image. He had cut his long hair, and was now wearing a bandana along with his goatee.

The match went back and forth between the two men. First Agassi took a set, then Sampras. The third went to a tiebreaker. Sampras was leading by two, but then let Agassi get ahead and finally win 7-6. After that, Sampras seemed to give out, and Agassi took the last set 6-4.

It had been a brutal tournament for Sampras. He had been feeling intense emotional strain over Gullikson's condition. After it was over, he was gracious in defeat, acknowledging Agassi's strength as a player. Agassi's return of serve, he said, was the best in the world. He predicted a rivalry between the two of them. "Tennis has been missing a rivalry. Andre and I could be a great one."

The next big tournament was the French Open. Sampras decided that if he wanted to finally win in France, it would help to get as much playing time as possible on clay before the Open. That spring he leapt into the European clay-court season and also signed up for Davis Cup competition in Italy.

But his plan backfired. Of the four European tournaments he played in, he lost in the first round three times. He had to retire from the fourth with a twisted ankle. When he got to France, catastrophe awaited. He lost there in the first round to a low-seeded Austrian named Gilbert Schaller.

"My whole clay-court season has been a disaster," he admitted.

To make matters worse, the loss meant that Agassi moved past him in world ranking, displacing Pete from the No. 1 position he had been fighting to hold on to. Then in March, he lost his Lipton hard court title to Agassi as well.

It was a very difficult time for Sampras. "This was the first time in my life I could ever remember feeling like that. I was down. The year wasn't going well. At that point it really seemed like it was all rolling downhill. Losing in the Australian final, dealing with Tim's situation, not playing well on the clay . . ."

Back in Tampa, Sampras tried to regroup before he returned to Europe to play at Wimbledon. Gullikson was undergoing chemotherapy. He and Pete talked almost daily on the telephone. Gullikson coached Sampras over the phone, urging him to go to Wimbledon with a new attitude.

The coaching seemed to work. Sampras's play was energetic and he moved through his opponents with a minimum of effort until he got to the finals. The few sets he lost to Brasch, Palmer and Matsuoka set the British press off in a flurry of predictions about his doom. But the announcements of his professional death were premature.

It had looked for a while like he'd be playing against Agassi again, but at the last minute Agassi lost the semi-final match to Boris Becker. Going up against Becker was something Sampras looked forward to. Becker was a great grass player, and a favorite of the Wimbledon crowd. Both athletes played well, but in the end Sampras played better. He out aced Becker 23-16 and swept the match in straight sets.

Surprisingly, the English crowd, ever resistant to Pete Sampras's extraordinary skill, gave a greater round of applause to the loser, Becker, than to the victor. It was typical of Pete's treatment by the English, but he didn't let it bother him. The victory was his and he dedicated it to Tim Gullikson. He had made history and he wanted it known that much of the credit went to his coach. They called it a "three-Pete"—winning the Wimbledon title three years in row. No matter how bad the rest of the year had been, Wimbledon turned it around for Sampras. Now he could get on with winning back his U.S. Open title.

When he found himself a few months later playing in the U.S. Open final against Andre Agassi, even Sampras must have admitted it was perfect. The rivalry that Sampras had predicted in Australia had been steadily building between the two players all year. The media fueled it. TV commercials showed them jumping out of taxicabs and setting up tennis nets in the middle of city streets, then launching into rallies. The message was obvious—they just couldn't wait to play each other.

As with all good rivalries, there was even a budding friendship and public statements of mutual respect. In Cincinnati that summer during the hard court tournament, when Agassi found out it was Sampras's 24th birthday, he arranged for a cake and a party at the hotel.

Going into the Open, things looked better for Agassi than for Sampras. After his Wimbledon victory, Sampras seemed to slack off. He lost the Cincinnati tournament in the quarterfinal match, and then lost the Indianapolis tournament in the semi-final. Agassi, meanwhile, was racking up victory after victory. Shortly before the Open, Agassi beat Sampras in a tournament in Montreal.

On top of all that, Sampras was faced with new worries about Tim Gullikson. Gullikson's health was getting worse. He had hoped to attend the U.S. Open to cheer Pete on, but then had to cancel when he had to start a new round of chemotherapy. In addition to the worry about his friend, Sampras had to deal with the disappointment of not having him there.

The press hyped the tournament as a contest between Sampras and Agassi, as if they didn't both have to play a lot of tough tennis to get to the finals. Both players spoke out, trying to calm down the speculations, but it did little good.

As it turned out, in this case the press was right. Both players survived some tough preliminary matches to get to the finals. But get there they did. Sampras faced Jaime Yzaga, the man who had defeated him the previous year, in the second round.

This year, though, Sampras was in top condition, even if he hadn't been winning titles. Serving aces that were clocked up to 128 mph (206 km/h), Sampras bulldozed over the Peruvian player in 92 minutes, 6-1, 6-4, 6-3. After that, Mark Philippoussis, Todd Martin, and Jim Courier all fell to the Sampras onslaught.

The final match with Agassi was a tough one. Hitting strong serves and volleys, Sampras finally won the first two sets. But then Agassi fought back to win the third.

The crowd was behind Agassi, cheering when they thought he might come from behind. But Sampras was unfazed. He got into a groove, at one point serving four aces in a row. Even so, Agassi fought it to a tiebreaker before he went down 7-5.

Sampras had won back his U.S. Open title. It was also his second Grand Slam title in a row. What had started out as a bad year, with the losses in Australia and France, had turned into a good one. Even though Agassi still held the No. 1 world ranking, at the age of 24 Sampras had collected seven Grand Slam titles, tying him with John McEnroe. He had five to go to reach the record set by Roy Emerson, but he still had a lot of time to do it.

Before the annual round of Grand Slam events

started again, however, another competition beckoned. Tim Gullikson's brother, Tom, asked Pete to play for the U.S. in the Davis Cup competition in December. The tournament was against the Russians.

Pete drew Andrei Chesnokov to open. It was a hard-played match. The Russian took the first set and Sampras the next two. Then when he was about to close it out, Pete somehow let the Russian take the fourth set in a tiebreaker, 6-7. That meant going to a fifth set during which Sampras started to cramp up. He fought off the pain to win the final set 6-4, but just after the match ended he collapsed in pain, his muscles knotting up uncontrollably, and had to be helped off the court.

Having beaten Jim Courier in straight sets and seeing Sampras's collapse as a sign of weakness, the Russians, and especially Yevgeny Kafelnikov, started boasting publicly about a Russian win. But Sampras insisted on playing doubles, and Gullikson substituted him for Richey Reneberg. Teamed up with Todd Martin in a rare doubles appearance, Sampras led the attack. The Russians lost in three straight.

That left the final singles match between Sampras and Kafelnikov, who was still boasting about how he would beat the American. But when push came to shove, it wasn't to be. Even with a sore hamstring, Sampras overwhelmed the Russian, winning the match in three sets.

Pete was the first American to win three matches on a Davis Cup weekend since John McEnroe had done it 13 years before. Even more important for Pete, he had done it on clay. The Americans now had the Davis Cup back. He had made up for the disaster the year before in Sweden.

There was other good news, too, when he regained his No. 1 world ranking, making 1995 the third year in a row Pete Sampras had ended the year as No. 1.

Chapter Seven

Collecting Slams

If 1995 started off badly for Pete Sampras, 1996 wasn't much better. Tim Gullikson was still undergoing chemotherapy, and things didn't look hopeful. Going into the Australian Open and the beginning of the new tour year, Sampras had to deal with all the memories from the year before when Gullikson had first gotten sick.

On top of that, Sampras also had a bad cold. After winning the first two rounds, he went up against Pete Philippoussis, an Australian player of Greek heritage. Philipoussis came on strong, acing Sampras 29 times to win the match in three sets.

It was definitely a bad start to the year. Not only was this the first time he had lost a Grand Slam event in straight sets since 1993, the loss meant that his No. 1 ranking went to Andre Agassi, who then lost it to Thomas Muster.

Talking about his loss, Sampras identified part of the problem as the Davis Cup. He was exhausted both mentally and physically after his performance against the Russians, and there just wasn't enough time to recover between the events. That led him to beg off the next Davis Cup competitions.

The first weekend in May, Pete's girlfriend Delaina Mulcahy graduated from law school. She and Pete had been planning to attend her graduation and celebrate her remarkable accomplishment when the news came that Tim Gullikson had died. Instead of celebrating, Pete went into mourning. He and Delaina traveled to Wheaton, Illinois, for the funeral. Pete was a pallbearer. He set his 1993 Wimbledon trophy next to Gullikson's coffin.

The loss of his coach and friend was devastating for Sampras. "We were together for three years," he said later. "It was like a marriage. When I was playing, I knew what he was thinking; when I did something wrong, I knew what he was going to say. We went through a lot. . . . There is an empty seat in the stand. I miss him terribly."

After the funeral, Sampras cancelled his appearance at the Italian Open. He also announced that he might miss the French Open as well. As the event approached, however, he changed his mind.

He also changed his strategy. In 1995, he had thought he might have a better chance in the French

Open if he played a lot on clay before the big tournament. The result was a disaster, as he got wiped out in the first round. In 1996 he announced that he would play the French tournament on his terms. That meant he went into the tournament having played only one other match on clay all year.

Of all the Grand Slam events, the French Open was the only one that still eluded Sampras. Winning it would be a big deal.

And it seemed he might. In the first round he served 23 aces against Magnus Gustafsson. That set the tone, and he went on to win matches against Seri Burguera, Todd Martin, Scott Draper, and Jim Courier. In the semi-final round he went up against his opponent from December's Davis Cup, Yevgeny Kafelnikov. After losing a bitterly fought first set in a tiebreak, Sampras seemed to just give up, as if he couldn't take any more. The next two sets went quickly to Kafelnikov, 6-0, 6-2.

It was a humiliating defeat for someone of Sampras's stature. Tom Gullikson thought that Sampras had "hit the wall." Sampras himself claimed he was fatigued.

But others were less generous in their judgements, arguing that he just quit. Given all that Sampras had been through in the previous month—the death of Tim, his friend and coach, the funeral—it was perhaps understandable. But it seemed like a terrible waste.

Never had he been so close to victory at the French Open; never had the defeat been so bitter.

During an interview after one of the matches, a reporter asked Sampras about Tim Gullikson. Pete broke down sobbing. He was exhausted when he headed back to Florida—so exhausted that he withdrew from the Queen's Club grass tournament in London. He didn't look that good at Wimbledon, either, at least in the beginning. He almost dumped his first round match. He seemed to get his bearings then, taking the next three matches.

But when he went into the quarterfinals against Richard Krajicek, it began to look like the French Open all over again. Krajicek won the first set, a bitterly fought tiebreaker. Sampras was behind and looking dejected. He lost the second set in another tiebreaker. Then the match had to be called because the ground had gotten soaked with rain.

The next day, they took it up again. But nothing had changed. Sampras went down in the third set 6-4, losing his Wimbledon title and breaking his three-year streak.

That fall Sampras and Delaina Mulcahy broke up after seven years together. Neither has spoken about what happened, but some say Mulcahy wanted to get married and Sampras did not. They had talked about it for years, but finally Mulcahy demanded an answer. When Pete still refused to get married, Mulcahy left and moved back to Houston, leaving Sampras alone in his big house in Tampa.

Pete had planned to play in the Olympics that summer, but pulled his hamstring while jogging and had to withdraw. That left only the U.S. Open among the big tournies in 1996. Sampras had been skunked in all the other Grand Slam tournaments. Everything now hung on that one event. And he pulled it out when he needed it, beating Michael Chang in the finals in straight sets. As it happened, the match was played on what would have been Tim Gullikson's 45th birthday.

"I was thinking about Tim all day today," Sampras said. "I still felt his spirit and even though he's not with us he's still very much in my heart. I wouldn't be a champion if it wasn't for his help."

The U.S. Open victory saved 1996 from being a complete disaster. Along with the minor tournaments Sampras won, it was enough to guarantee the No. 1 ranking he so desired as the year closed. It was the fourth year in a row he ended the year as No. 1. He would hold that position over the next two years as well, running his streak to six consecutive years.

In the years that followed, Pete continued to heal from the loss of his coach and to apply himself to his goal of surpassing Roy Emerson's record of 12 Grand Slam victories. He has managed to win at least one every year. In 1997 he recovered his Wimbledon title—

his fourth Wimbledon championship. He also won the Australian Open again. In 1998, he successfully defended that title, making him a five-time champion, though he lost the other three big events. At the end of 1998, still ranked No. 1 in the world, he was only one victory shy of tying Emerson's record.

As 1999 opened, Sampras elected not to play in the Australian Open, choosing instead to vacation in Hawaii with his new girlfriend, actress Kimberley Williams. He and Williams had met in April of 1997 in a date set up by Sampras's friend Kevin O'Keefe and a friend of Williams. On their first date they went hiking near Los Angeles. On a later date they went to a U2 concert in Las Vegas. Williams flew to England to be with Pete during the 1997 Wimbledon tournament.

The decision not to enter the Australian Open took many by surprise. Sampras claimed he was tired and needed a break. Some people suspected, though, that with only one Grand Slam win needed to tie Roy Emerson's record, Sampras didn't want to do it in Australia. He'd already won the Australian Open three times. There was nothing new for him there.

There was one event left, however, that still eluded him—the French Open. As he's grown older, it has become more important. To finally win that tournament, and to make it his 12th victory, would have been a wonderful accomplishment.

However, it wasn't to be in 1999. In an echo of his 1998 performance, he lost in the second round to 100th-ranked Ukrainian player Andrei Medvedev. With his continuing difficulties with the courts at Roland Garros, it seemed unlikely that Sampras would ever put together the Grand Slam he just missed in 1994. But when he was asked if he would give up his quest, he replied firmly, "I'm *never* going to give up."

Despite his problems with the French Open, Pete went on to win at Wimbledon for the sixth straight time. In an all-American final against Andre Agassi on the fourth of July, he won convincingly in three straight sets. The victory was his 12th Grand Slam win, tying Emerson's record.

Clearly, Pete Sampras still has time left to garner more titles and more honors. A real fighter and a real gentleman, Pete Sampras will continue to thrill tennis fans for years to come.

Glossary of Tennis Terms

ace — a point scored by the server, when the opponent is unable to touch, or barely touches, the ball served. It flies past.

backhand — a stroke from the side of the body opposite the side the player normally serves from (left side for a right-handed server). Two-handed backhand means the player uses both hands to hold the racket and deliver the shot.

baseliner — a player who plays from the back of the court, near the baseline, usually using ground strokes to keep the ball in play. This is generally considered a steady, safer way to play tennis, but can still require power.

court — area on which tennis is played. A tennis court is 78 feet (23.77 meters) long and 36 feet (10.97 meters) wide. The baseline is the back line of the court on both sides. The sideline for singles play and service is 4 1/2 feet (1.37 meters) inside the doubles sideline. The court may be made of differing surfaces — among them hard (perhaps asphalt or concrete), clay, carpet or grass. The way the players move and the way the ball bounces in play varies according to the court surfaces. Some players tend to play better on one surface.

crosscourt — a shot that travels diagonally across the court.

deuce — a tie score in a game, where both players have 40 points (40-all). The first point taken after deuce is called advantage, either for the server, "advantage server," or the receiver, "advantage receiver." At deuce, one of the players must get two points in a row to win. In the spectacular 1995 Wimbledon final, Arantxa Sanchez Vicario lost to Steffi Graf after 13 deuces.

drop shot — a shot aimed to just clear the net, and fall close to the net, when the opponent is playing near the baseline. Such a shot may win the point or force the opponent to race to the net.

fault — an infraction of the rules of play of tennis. A fault is called when a player's serve hits the net, or the ball served falls outside the opposite service court. If the server steps on the baseline, or misses hitting the ball during the serve, that too is a fault. If a server commits two faults in a row that is a double fault and she loses a point.

game — smallest division of a tennis match . The first player to win six games and be two games ahead wins the set. The points in a game are called love, 15, 30, 40, advantage, and game. The server's score is mentioned first, except in games that reach a tie. For example, when the server wins the first point in a game, the score is 15-0 (fifteen-love). When the server loses the first point, the score is 0-15 (love-fifteen). When ties occur, the score is 15-all, 30-all, or deuce (40-all).

Grand Slam — winning all of the four major championships in tennis: the Australian Open, French Open, Wimbledon, and the US Open. Also a descriptive term for these events.

ground stroke — any shot a player uses to hit the ball back after the ball has bounced once on the court.

International Tennis Federation (ITF) — the world governing body of tennis, controlling most amateur matches and the major professional championships. About 100 countries belong to the ITF.

lob — a shot hit high in the air. It is intended to go over the head of the opponent.

love — the scoring word for zero points.

match — the overall tennis contest, including a number of sets.

majors — the four most important championships in tennis each year: The Australian Open, French Open, Wimbledon and the US Open. Also known as the Big Four. Sometimes these are called Grand Slam events, too. If a player wins all four in one calendar year, she has made a Grand Slam.

overhead smash — a hard stroke swung at the ball from above the head, like a serve.

rally — an extended exchange of strokes between players.

seeding — a ranking list of tennis players. The strongest players are seeded first, and so on. Then tournaments are set up so that strong players do not play one another in the early rounds. This keeps the stars in the tournament longer.

set — a division of a tennis match consisting of a number of games. The first player to win at least six games, and be ahead of her opponent by two games, wins the set. Most tournaments now use tie breakers when the score becomes tied at six games all. The player who wins two out of three sets wins the match.

straight sets — two sets won in a row. When a player wins two sets in a row, she has won the match, since two out of three sets is a win. Winning in straight sets is often a short and decisive victory, showing the strength of the winner's game.

tie breaker — a play-off at six games all to prevent long, drawn-out matches. Before the introduction of the tie breaker, there was no limit to the number of games that could be played in a set. In a tie breaker a player must be the first to reach at least 6 points, and be ahead by two points, in order to win the set.

volley — any shot that hits the ball during play, before the ball has bounced on the court. Most volleys are made close to the net and are meant to be quick winners. The net player risks losing the point to a high lob that goes over her head and lands just inside the baseline.

Research Sources

Branham H. A. *Sampras : A Legend in the Works.*
Chicago: Bonus Books, 1996.

Miller, Calvin Craig. *Pete Sampras.* (Great Athletes
Series.) Greensboro: Morgan Reynolds, 1998.

Rambeck, Richard, and James R. Rothaus. *Pete
Sampras.* Plymouth, Minn.: Childs World, 1996.

Sherrow, Victoria. *Sports Great Pete Sampras.*
Springfield, NJ: Enslow Publishers, Inc, 1996.

Look for these other

CHAMPION SPORT
BIOGRAPHIES

Tennis
- Martina Hingis

Soccer
- Maradona
- Ronaldo

Formula One Racing
- Michael Schumacher
- Jacques Villeneuve

Basketball
- Michael Jordan
- Shaquille O'Neal

Boxing
- Muhammad Ali

Figure Skating
- Tara Lipinski

We hoped you enjoyed reading this book. We welcome your comments. Please contact us:

Warwick Publishing
162 John Street, 3rd Floor
Toronto, Ontario, Canada
M5V 2E5

Telephone: (416) 596-1555

FAX: (416) 596-1520

Website: www.warwickgp.com

E-mail: mbrooke@warwickgp.com